FIVE
PRIMITIVE MASTERS

FIVE

PRIMITIVE MASTERS

Wilhelm Uhde

ARNO PRESS * NEW YORK

A PUBLISHING AND LIBRARY SERVICE OF THE NEW YORK TIMES

Arno Series of Contemporary Art No. 35
Reprinted with the permission of Lee A. Ault
Library of Congress Catalog Card No. 75-91371
Manufactured in the United States of America
by Arno Press, New York, 1969

mvnd
5-17

WILHELM UHDE

FIVE PRIMITIVE MASTERS

TRANSLATED

BY

RALPH THOMPSON

THE QUADRANGLE PRESS

NEW YORK M·C·M·I·L

When I first decided to write this book, I had a scholarly and rather ambitious plan in mind. For years I had been accumulating factual material on the artists in question, and I intended to give a chronological account of the life of each and the fullest possible catalogue of their works.

But circumstances prevented my carrying out this design. Returning to Paris at the end of the second World War, I found that my file of biographical notes, critical memoranda, reproductions, etc., had disappeared during the Occupation. To begin all over again would have taken a great deal of time—quite possibly more time than I still had at my disposal. There was nothing left to do except to renounce my original plan, and to content myself with a discussion of the most important aspects of each career, using as a primary source my own impressions and recollections. It follows that the present book is less factual and more subjective than would otherwise have been the case. Nevertheless, the art historian who may later write a formal history of the group will find here hints and details that should lighten his labors considerably.

Of the five artists discussed, Rousseau, Vivin and Séraphine are now dead. I knew them well during their latter years, and the other two, Bombois and Bauchant, are still my good friends. My feeling is that these five, because of their singular simplicity and self-dedication, form a group of their own within the wider circle of modern Primitive art.

I have written of them before—in articles for magazines, in my book *Picasso et la Tradition Française*, and in the *Histoire de l'Art Contemporain*, edited by René Huyghe and Germain Bazin. These earlier comments are summed up and given something like final form here, although the bulk of the text is now first published. Much of the chapter on the Douanier, however, is taken, with minor changes, from my *Henri Rousseau*, which was published in France by Eugène Figuière in 1911 and which helped to establish the Douanier's fame. It later appeared in two German editions and was heavily drawn upon, when the French edition was out of print, for the major Rousseau monographs.

Collector, critic, dealer and historian, Wilhelm Uhde (1874-1947) was born in Germany but spent most of his adult life in France. Among his books are the aforementioned *Henri Rousseau* (Paris, 1911), pioneer work of its kind; *Picasso et la Tradition Française* (Paris, 1928); and an autobiography, *Von Bismarck bis Picasso* (Zurich, 1938). Uhde was reading proof on the present work in its original edition (Zurich, 1947) the day before he died.

WILHELM UHDE: PARIS 1947

INTRODUCTION

Our century has witnessed the flowering of an extraordinary group of artists in France. Not the least extraordinary thing about the group is that its members remained total strangers to one another. Normally, an art group, or school, consists of friends and associates—or, at any rate, of leaders and disciples. The members of the Impressionist school, for example, were inspired by a common purpose and devoted to a common program. They produced pictures that still testify to their artistic communion; indeed, signatures alone show whether certain early Impressionist paintings are by Monet, Sisley, Pissarro or Renoir.

It is quite another story with the artists we are discussing. They had no group experimental "purpose," no group "program." There was no "leader," nor were there "disciples." Each worked alone and was quite unaware of the others. The style of each is so distinctive as to be immediately recognizable. In time, to be sure, the reputation of Henri Rousseau, the eldest, became general. But about all his success could have connoted to the rest was that they too, since they too were self-taught, poor and obscure, might by some remote chance become famous. We are discussing, in brief, a group of individualists. They form a "group" in the sense that the early Christian saints, for all their isolated private lives, formed a spiritual brotherhood.

What specifically do these artists have in common? They were all of humble origin, but this has little bearing on the question. Watteau was once a roofer's apprentice, born to much the same social handicaps, yet he developed into an entirely different sort of artist. They were all self-taught, but the history of art is full of examples of self-taught painters who resembled neither one another nor the five here under consideration.

Coming fresh to the work of these five, the uninitiated observer will probably be struck first of all by an air of unsophisticated artlessness or clumsiness, and may well conclude that the only quality common to the group is precisely this artlessness. Its presence, of course, can hardly be denied. But the initiate will recognize it for what it is: an inevitable but relatively unimportant aspect of the group character. Certainly he will refuse to attribute it to social naiveté or lack of training alone. Charles Péguy once noted that the difference between genius and talent is a matter not so much of training as of inspiration, and went on to discuss the frequent ineptitude of true geniuses and the consequent "obvious clumsiness" of much of their work. If Péguy is right, we may ask whether the ineptitude of our artists is not also that of geniuses whose talents happened to be limited in particular respects.

It was Paul Valéry who said that he would rather create a poor thing in the hard, cold light of reason than a masterpiece in a so-called elevated or ecstatic state of mind. Thus he marked himself unmistakably as a champion of talent. Henri Matisse and Jean Cocteau, among others, would doubtless agree with him; and, in truth, it is difficult to discover any "obvious clumsiness" in the work of these three men. Plato, nevertheless, understood the mystery of genius (and Péguy followed his example), defining reason as merely mortal, ecstasy as godlike and divine. Talent is a product of reason. Genius is intuitive, the product of heart and soul, not of mind.

In the work of many artists the two are blended, but there are also special cases. Matisse and Cocteau, I should say, have talent and no genius; Péguy has genius and no talent. And likewise with our artists: most of their work is the expression of heart and soul, uncomplicated by mind, and thus akin to the wisdom of nature, to the universal pulse, to the music of the spheres. Mere talent as such could contribute nothing to the essential meaning of their work. Its true content is the emotional richness of their inner lives.

Their outer lives were far from rich, lacking almost all the privileges and creature comforts that numberless others take for granted. More often than not, when I myself have been downcast, the Champs Elysées *lay only a few blocks distant; a leisurely stroll under its trees and perhaps a chat with old friends met on the way, and life for me became bright once more. Occasionally, when ailing, I have been able to pack up and travel south, to bask in the sun and stare out at the sea. Or when merely peevish, I knew that the Louvre was nearby and that an hour or so spent with the Italian Primitives, Poussin, Manet or Corot and I should be set right again and my impatience put to shame.*

So too with the rank and file of artists. Music, sculpture, literature, philosophy—all manner of precious things are usually theirs for the asking. If they will, they may immerse themselves in the art of the past for comfort and stimulation. Their own art, however "personal" and "original," is nurtured by education and long centuries of cultural tradition.

But Rousseau, Vivin, Bauchant, Bombois and Séraphine lived and worked in another world. They had no education to speak of, no opportunities, no cultural stimulus, no funds. People of their world do not saunter along the Champs Elysées or lounge on sunny beaches beside the Mediterranean. The sunshine they knew best filtered like charity into their gloomy rooms for a brief moment and then was gone. Occasional visits to the Louvre, if they made them, had little effect on their careers; the masterpieces of art, as it were, spoke another language. And to whom could they themselves speak in their own language about their own pictures? Their friends were the man or woman next door, the cafe-keeper down the street, the grocer on the corner—all as circumscribed as they. Year in, year out, their lives wore a humdrum pattern and ran in humdrum channels. The business of earning enough for mere bread and wine came first, and luxury, like as not, consisted of cheap magazines or picture postcards. Picture postcards and magazine illustrations, as it happens, were one source of the art of Rousseau and Vivin.

A miraculous state of affairs, when one stops to consider it: the creation of beauty out of squalor, inner riches out of external need. There are innumerable men and women who, given every conceivable advantage and encouragement, can create nothing at all. Rousseau was so poor that sometimes he played his fiddle for pennies in the street; his horizon of experience extended barely beyond the old fortifications of Paris. Vivin's extended barely beyond the dingy walls of a two-room flat. Bombois was a day laborer, chipping away at paving stones. Bauchant was a peasant behind the plow. Séraphine tended cattle and scrubbed floors. The achievement of these artists is not in the least diminished by its having been wrought with clumsy hands. Of course the hands were clumsy. They were not only hands of genius but plebeian hands, as well.

Emotional verity, not clumsiness, is the prime common quality of their work. Quite true: their work is not in the magnificent tradition of Rome, Madrid and Amsterdam, which suggests the power and glory of man. It is rather in the modest tradition of Florence, Ferrara and Bruges, which proclaims the power and glory of God. Ecstasy and devotion are its earmarks; it is infused with elements of the universal and divine. It is inspired interpretation, not classic representation—an art of essences, not surfaces. Our five painted what their hearts, rather than tradition or teachers, taught them to paint.

HENRI ROUSSEAU

One Sunday, years before the first World War, I pushed my way through the crowds on the Rue de la Gaîté, a bustling Left Bank street lined with playhouses and primitive cinemas and thronged with artists, tradesmen and apaches in a holiday mood. Leaving the Rue de la Gaîté, I crossed the Avenue du Maine into the narrower, quieter Rue Vercingétorix, which runs southwest across the Plaisance quarter out toward the fortifications of Paris. Then I turned right into a deserted little side-street only a few steps long and ending abruptly in a blank wall. This was, and is, the Rue Perrel.

In those days a plaster-molder had a studio on the ground floor of one of the Rue Perrel's rickety houses. Upstairs were rooms which he rented out. A sign outside one of the rooms read: *Lessons in Diction, Music, Painting, Singing (Solfège)*. I knocked and walked in.

Henri Rousseau himself came to the door, taking both my hands in his and welcoming me in a voice as gentle and guileless as a child's. This was one of his "at homes," and he was not wearing his usual paint-smudged smock. A number of guests were jammed into the little room —typical neighborhood bourgeois, for the most part, accustomed to chicken once a week and *pot-au-feu* the rest, but also a few outsiders, including a couple of professional artists and a writer nobody ever heard of. Most of the crowd was gathered around an easel, looking at a picture. The picture was almost as large as the room itself—a weird primeval-jungle scene, with exotic vegetation and lurking wild beasts.

"Well," Rousseau said to a solemn-looking man dressed in black, "what's your opinion?" There was a faintly insistent note in the question, as though he had already asked it once and had no reply. The solemn-looking man hemmed and hawed, but finally handed down his verdict:

15

"Rousseau, I'll tell you. That picture of yours in the last Independent show wasn't half bad, either." Whereupon someone else broke in to ask why the foliage in the foreground wasn't darker, and a third remarked that it was plenty dark enough. A general argument ensued, with comments and criticisms from all sides.

Rousseau, meanwhile, turned to a young man who stood staring at the picture, apparently oblivious to the debate. "Well, my friend, what do *you* think?" Again I was struck by the simple charm of the Douanier's voice.

"It's good," the young man answered. "It's beautiful. In fact, I think it's the most beautiful thing you've ever done."

"Ah then, it will be all right?" It was very important that it be all right, for the young man was a collector and had commissioned the picture. It was so very all right that he wanted to take it home with him then and there, but Rousseau refused. He explained that he had decided to change certain details, and then wanted to hang the picture in the coming *Salon d'Automne*.

He was, though, proud and pleased. At last he was getting occasional commissions, and he was sure the number would increase. His guests in general were also pleased, for here it was a leisurely Sunday, and there was wine to drink, and by their presence they were demonstrating that they knew something about art—perhaps more than their host himself. They lifted their glasses as someone called for a toast to Henri Rousseau.

★　　★

Sitting along the wall was an old man who took no part in the ceremony. Instead, he gazed moodily out of the window, as though he found the subject of painting a bore and the assembled guests a lot of dolts. He was a former colleague of Rousseau's in the municipal toll service, like him a retired *gabelou* (Rousseau had never been in the national customs service and hence was not, strictly speaking, a *douanier*). He figured that he knew the host better than anyone else in the room.

16

What is more, he didn't think much of him . . . After all, what could you expect? Rousseau had been next to worthless in the service. He had never been allowed to do anything that required brains. His job had been to hang around the quai like a watchman, keeping an eye on the barges. How could you have trusted him with a more responsible job? To begin with, he believed in spirits and spooks. One evening, for example, the boys had rigged up a skeleton between wine barrels in the warehouse and jiggled it with a string. Along had come Rousseau, and what had he done? Instead of acting like a normal man, he had politely asked the damned thing whether it would like a drink!

What a simpleton! Besides, Rousseau had always been the silent sort, never willing to say much about anything or anybody. He had preferred to sneak off somewhere alone and fiddle with his pictures and paints. It had been the same wherever he was stationed—at the Pont de la Tournelle, out at the fortifications, at the Porte de Meudon.

No great loss to the service when the day came for him to quit! He ought to feel honored that someone who had really done a decent job and earned his wages would come to see him at all. That crackpot an artist? Let nobody waste good breath spouting such nonsense! Why, practically everyone except "Americans" laughed at Rousseau's pictures (he called all foreigners "Americans"), and who didn't know that "Americans" were easy marks? They fell for everything, and would "collect" anything, from royal cigar butts to a half-wit's so-called art! Rousseau an artist? Well, well! . . . The old man sniffed contemptuously, and took a good slug of wine from his glass.

The years rolled by. Rousseau continued to paint. The pictures on his easel grew richer and mellower; he himself grew grayer and more stooped. Yet whenever I came to call, there sat the same old man on the same chair, as contemptuous as ever—a perfect symbol of the great philistine public whose scorn and indifference have always broken artists' hearts.

★ ★

Rousseau had a good deal of company, at that, for he knew many people and liked to entertain. The cot he slept in would be folded and stuck in a corner. His chairs would be arrayed as precisely as a squad of soldiers around the walls of the room. On the floor lay the cheap carpet a shopkeeper had let him have in exchange for three of his pictures. Jugs of wine stood waiting on the table. Guests of all types appeared, including almost always a lady with four daughters wearing flowers in their hair.

Likewise present, as a rule, were a number of Rousseau's art or music pupils. The eldest of these was 70-odd, and utterly untalented, but whenever asked how he was progressing, Rousseau would gravely answer, "He's coming along." Young painters and writers also showed up. Rousseau was interested in all the arts; painting was simply his favorite. He played the violin well, composed music, wrote poetry and plays. One of his plays, incidentally, he sent to the Comédie Française—which returned it, explaining politely that it would cost too much to produce.

His soirées were supposed to be literary-philosophical affairs, but there was always much drinking, laughter and horseplay. Whenever the atmosphere became a trifle bacchantic, the mother and her four daughters with flowers in their hair would make a ladylike exit. By midnight things were often bacchantic for fair—perhaps with old Rousseau himself in the midst of the chaos, tootling a flute before the full-length portrait of his dead wife, and dancing from foot to foot, the tears streaming from his eyes.

Most of the guests had a fine time at these parties, and probably only Rousseau's younger music pupils didn't find them exciting enough. For them, his so-called Examination Days were much more so. On such occasions, the fond parents would take seats around the room, having first shaken hands with the *maître*. The *maître*, much wrought up, would be dressed in his best black suit with the violet ribbon of the *Palmes Académiques* in his buttonhole (he had once taught drawing in a municipal school, and had been thus rewarded by the authorities).

At last all was ready, and the examinations would begin. But they were soon concluded, for none of the pupils performed as expected. Some played the wrong selections, others deliberately wrong notes. Rousseau's pupils teased him endlessly, and could think up a new trick every day. Once they invited a group of people Rousseau didn't know to a soirée he hadn't planned. The arrival of the first two or three delighted the old man, for he felt that if strangers came to call, he must be getting famous. But the fourth guest made him wonder, and for the tenth he wouldn't even open the door.

Rousseau was in fact a great innocent, with little knowledge of the wiles of the world. His instinct was to believe that everybody was as honest as he, and in one case above all (as will appear) he was tragically mistaken. He looked for the good in people, and overlooked everything else, whether it was what they did for a living or even more obvious traits and facts. I, for example, was fairly young when we first met. One day I happened to make a remark that a young man would ordinarily not have made. From that moment forward Rousseau assumed that I was some thirty years older than I actually was. He talked of the days when we both had been boys. He asked a woman patently my senior whether she was my daughter, and a full-grown man whether he was my son. So little did he know of life in general. As for the little we know of his life, that may be quickly summarized.

★   ★

He was born in Laval, Department of Mayenne, in 1844, the son of a tinsmith. His mother is said to have been so excessively pious that she spent far more than the family could afford on delicacies to give the local clergy when they came to call. I do not believe—as I used to—the story about Rousseau's going to Mexico in the 1860's as a regimental musician in Maximilian's army. He was, however, a sergeant during the Franco-Prussian war, and claimed to have seen some front-line action.

Settling in Paris after the war, he entered the municipal toll service and began to paint in his spare time. There are a number of stories about how he happened to take up painting in the first place. According to one, he was urged to it by Alfred Jarry ("Père Ubu"), who also came from Laval and whose father had been a friend of Rousseau's father. According to another, Gauguin is supposed to have made a bet that any completely naive person could paint if given a chance—and having met Rousseau, started him off. It is needless to argue whether such stories are true or false. Rousseau's sense of artistic mission was so strong that he required no external stimulus. It is commonly believed that he was 40 or 41 when he began—*i.e.*, that he began about 1885. But works dating from this period are technically so skilled that it may be taken for granted that he started earlier.

Earlier than that, at any rate, he fell in love with a Polish girl whom he idealized in a late picture, "The Dream," as Yadwigha. He married twice, and long outlived his second wife. By the first he had a daughter. She was taken from him at the age of about 15 and brought up elsewhere, for in his innocence he played the bachelor much too freely in her presence.

Always poor, he tried to eke out a living in various ways. For a time he made transcripts for a lawyer. Soon after leaving the toll service, he opened a little shop in which his wife sold pens, pencils, writing paper and his pictures. He entered (unsuccessfully) a prize competition for the decoration of public buildings, and once drafted plans for an academy which was to be under his direction.

Despite his poverty, he found time to help others, and for a while served as an unpaid social worker and charity canvasser, going from door to door to collect alms. For himself he was content with little, and toward others more than generous. He once told a photographer who had reproduced one of his paintings, "I can't afford to pay you in cash, but come around tomorrow and I'll give you six pictures for your trouble." It should be borne in mind that he treasured his pictures above anything in the world. As for the photographer, he couldn't be bothered to fetch the six he had been promised—a decision he regretted later on. There are people who go through life as though they were special guests on earth; and then there are those whose joy is to give, rather than receive. These latter are few and far between. One of them was Henri Rousseau.

He earned a little cash by selling landscapes to his Plaisance neighbors, or by now and then doing a portrait for a small fee. One of his most charming portraits is that of a chubby child with a lapful of flowers. This child stands on the lawn of a park or garden and holds up its dress in front with one hand and dangles a puppet from the other. Rousseau received 300 francs for this portrait, which is the largest sum, I believe, he ever received for a painting. The child's parents couldn't afford even that, and had to relinquish the picture in settlement of a small laundry bill. On the whole, like most other artists, Rousseau did his best work when best paid. Whoever tried to take advantage of him money-wise—paying him in more or less worthless goods rather than in cash—as a rule got a less interesting picture. Rousseau was not always as simple as he seemed.

For years he exhibited his work at the annual *Salon des Indépendants*. It was the Independents who made his name known, and he who helped advertise them, in turn. For his pictures became the great attraction there, and Paris crowded in to look and laugh for two months every year. Curiosity-seekers craned their necks at his pictures as though at some comic incident on the boulevards; perfect strangers nudged one another and fell into friendly talk. I never heard such laughter, even at a circus, as when Rousseau's "The Sovereigns" went on display. Any one who suggested that the work might have artistic merits would have been rushed off to the asylum at Charenton.

Now and then, however, along would come a young person who seemed to take Rousseau seriously. And, in fact, within a few years he had a place of honor at the *Salon d'Automne*. One of Maillol's handsomest sculptures stood in the middle of a small room, with a huge Rousseau jungle scene serving as background. This triumph had not been engineered. It was due simply to the virtues of the picture, and won the Douanier earnest admirers. The public began to ask why the Gobelins didn't reproduce his works in tapestry.

Now there were more commissions—as many as three or four at a time. He worked at his easel day and night. Just when everything seemed to be going beautifully, he made his tragic mistake. An unscrupulous acquaintance whispered in his ear that there was an easy way for both of them to make a great deal of money. In his naiveté Rousseau agreed, not realizing that his tempter was an out-and-out criminal. The upshot was that the old man was haled before a court of assizes, tried and convicted. His sentence remitted under the provisions of the *loi Bérenger*, he beamed with gratitude. "*Je vous remercie, Monsieur le Président,*" he told the judge; "*je ferai le portrait de votre dame.*"*

---

* "Thank you, your honor. I'll paint a portrait of your wife."

Picasso arranged a banquet for Rousseau once this unfortunate incident was closed.* The young artists who had become his especial admirers attended en masse and toasted the guest of honor at such length that eventually he fell asleep, overcome with the joys of the occasion.

★　　★

There was not much time for joy remaining. One evening he visited me in the ancient cloister on the Boulevard des Invalides in which I then made my home. The high windows were open wide to the breeze drifting in from the park across the way, and it was so dark I could scarcely see his features. But I gathered from an undertone in his voice that he was in a solemn mood. So he was. He fell to talking about war, and he hated war. "If a king tries to start a war," he declared with great gravity, "a mother should go to him and forbid it."

On July 14, 1910—the last *Quatorze Juillet* he lived to celebrate—I went to his room. There were other callers, and he was dressed for the holiday and on the point of pouring some wine. "Do you love peace?" he demanded, and when I said yes, we all drank to peace. Then he took me by the hand, led me to the window and pointed out the German flag—my native flag—fluttering among the others below.

On a hot August day a few weeks later I knocked at his door. Receiving no answer, I walked in. He lay on his bed, ghastly pale. There was a painful sore on his leg. He was so apathetic that he didn't even brush away the flies which buzzed around his face, but he did talk of getting up soon and going on with his painting. Some days after that, I came home to find a note saying that he was dying in the Necker Hospital and had begged me to come as soon as possible. I rushed there

---

* The *loi Bérenger,* under which Rousseau escaped jail, is an act for the relief of first offenders. Rousseau's accomplice, Sauvage by name, was one of his former music pupils and a clerk in the Bank of France. Persuading the old man to open an account under a pseudonym, he forged papers which indicated a sizable credit in this account, then paid Rousseau a small sum for his trouble and made off with the rest. Sauvage's sentence was five years. (*Tr.*)

HENRI ROUSSEAU: SELF PORTRAIT (THE NATIONAL MUSEUM, PRAGUE)

HENRI ROUSSEAU: PEASANT WEDDING

and found him sinking fast. For hours I sat by his bed, and he clasped my hand tightly. Two days later he died. He was 66 years old.

★   ★

With the death of Henri Rousseau, a precious spirit passed away. What made his life so precious and his death so great a loss? Was it his childlike candor, his innocence of the world and its compromises and evils? Was it that he embodied the words of the Gospel: "Blessed are the poor in spirit, for theirs is the kingdom of heaven"? Was it the fantasy and imagination embodied in his art, the tenderly heroic and refreshingly quixotic aspects of his nature?

All such questions, of course, will be answered differently by different men. I myself believe that Rousseau's greatest quality was greater than any of these. It was his emotional self-dedication, his endurance, his overwhelming love and passion for, and faith in, life. Rarely in any given century are there men of similar emotional force and conviction. Rousseau embraced life and art as though they were identical. He loved as only a great artist can love, and painted as only a great lover can paint.

His love was not the ordinary bourgeois sort—throbbing and intense in youth, then gradually relaxed, and finally quiescent. The passion pulsed hotly as long as he lived. His two marriages and various affairs expressed the deepest hunger of his soul as well as the urgency of his physical powers. To love and be loved was his great desire. He went through life bearing his heart in his hand as an offering. He wanted to marry every woman he met—and, significantly enough, usually testified to his love with the gift of a picture.

Even in his last years he wanted to marry, and chose a maiden lady of 54, daughter of a former colleague in the toll service. The woman wasn't interested, and her father concluded that Rousseau had become senile. But the Douanier would not be put off. He slaved at his painting to earn thousands of francs extra to buy her gifts; he haunted her doorstep. One day he begged her to arrange the publication of the banns. Hoping to be rid of him, she brusquely told him to go and do it himself.

Taking her at her word, Rousseau filed the necessary papers, and on the appointed day knocked at her door with the friend he had chosen as best man. The happy hour, he announced, had come.

"The happy hour for what?" she inquired coldly. "For our wedding," Rousseau answered. The woman flew into a rage and threw him out of the house. Later, as Rousseau wiped away the tears, his friend suggested that he ask the woman to return the valuable gifts he had given her. Rousseau wouldn't hear of it. He intended, he said, to keep the valuable gifts she had given him: snips of ribbon she had worn and other trifling mementos. "But she's turned you down," the friend reminded him; "what else can you do?" "I'll keep right on," Rousseau replied.

Which is exactly what he did do. Soon after his rebuff, he came to me and said he had a favor to ask. Would I please draw up a certificate to the effect that he was as intelligent as the next man and that I owned and admired a number of his pictures? I gather that he asked as much of other people he knew, then took the certificates to the woman's father, hoping still to convince him that he would make a suitable son-in-law. It was not in his character to admit defeat. Even as he lay dying, he sent tender messages to the woman—all in vain.

The desire to love and be loved, basic in human nature, is paralleled by the artist's yearning to create and achieve recognition as a creator. Rousseau gave more than 25 years of his life to his art. He gave every available moment, sleeping in his clothes to save time, even neglecting the sore that led to his death. During his last days in the hospital, no longer strong enough to eat, he still found strength to discuss a half-finished picture and to deplore the delay caused by his illness. He brought to bear on the entire course of his work that sort of intense and indefatigable purpose which most people summon up only at odd moments in their lives.

And as generously as he gave, he expected to take. As a man, he regarded the love of woman as his right; as an artist, he expected sympathetic understanding of his art. To him, fame was both necessary and inevitable. Doubtless the only paintings that really moved him were his own, but he respected all kinds—even the worst, since that was what the public most readily appreciated. The death of Bouguereau, for example, affected him deeply. He was sure that he himself was a major artist, and in all likelihood ranked himself among the greatest alive. It

HENRI ROUSSEAU: INDEPENDENCE DAY

HENRI ROUSSEAU: THE CHARIOT OF PERE JUNICT

seemed only logical to him that everybody else should feel more or less the same way.

This self-esteem was neither arrogant nor assumed. Few artists in history have been less arrogant and less assuming. When his dealer broached the subject of a regular financial subsidy, Rousseau was ready to settle for 20 francs a day, Sundays and holidays included—which for him represented affluence. One day an elderly gentleman knocked at the door, identified himself as Puvis de Chavannes and began to discuss the fine points of painting. Rousseau never realized that his caller was not the renowned Puvis at all, but an imposter, dressed up by waggish conspirators. He evinced no surprise, moreover, when he read in the paper that a "M. Rousseau" had won a silver medal, or when Gauguin told him that he had been awarded a government commission, or when he was informed that the President of the Republic expected him at a State reception.

On the contrary, he was astounded to discover that it was another Rousseau who had won the medal, that nobody in the Louvre knew anything about the government commission, and that the attendants at the Elysée refused to let him in. "I went up to the front door," he later explained to his friends, "but they told me that I couldn't get in without a card of invitation. When I insisted, the President himself came out, patted me on the back, and said, 'Sorry, Rousseau, but you see you're wearing an ordinary business suit. Since everybody else has on formal clothes, I can't very well receive you today. But come again some other time'."

With little lies like these he tried to bolster his wounded pride. He couldn't believe that anyone would laugh at him and his pictures. But eventually he discovered the truth, and saw that he would have to cope with the situation. He became less frank, confiding his thoughts to some friends but not to others. He began to adapt and alter facts so as to put himself in the best possible light. One thinks again of the Gospel: "Behold, I send you forth as sheep in the midst of wolves; be ye therefore wise as serpents and harmless as doves."

His passion for work, his will power, his unshakeable confidence—these set Rousseau apart from ordinary mortals. His faith in himself was so great that it became an inspiration to others. Unhappy, elderly neighborhood folk would come to his room and sit quietly in a corner, finding renewed hope in his very presence. There he would sit on a stool, working calmly away at a huge picture. If the afternoon happened to be warm, he might doze off for a few minutes, then awake with a start and go back to his painting. On one occasion, he turned to some visitors with a curious expression on his face. "Did you notice," he asked, "how my hand was moving?"

"Of course, Rousseau. You were filling in that color with your brush."

"No, no," he answered, "not I. My dead wife was just here and she guided my hand. Didn't you see her or hear her? 'Keep at it, Rousseau,' she whispered, 'you're going to make out all right after all'." He settled back on his stool and worked steadily until sunset. Who could laugh at such a man? Who could fail to envy his candor, tenacity and genius?

★ ★

Goethe once said that dilettantes never can see the difficulties inherent in an undertaking, and consequently are forever lightly trying things beyond their powers. Rousseau was no dilettante. He saw the difficulties clearly enough, and his career in art was a protracted struggle to overcome them. In a matter of 25 years, he poured more creative energy into the struggle than the average man expends in a lifetime.

His pictures were not lightly or idly done. They were not merely the fruit of leisure hours, of visits to museums, of placid reminiscences with friends. They were the product of his inmost vitality, shaped in the course of sleepless nights and arduous days before his easel. He was not simply a recorder; he was a creator. He painted with his whole life, his full heart, his full hopes. His character as an artist was as well-rounded and deep-rooted as a forest oak. It expressed his overpowering faith in the significances of nature and in his own destiny, not merely a desire to "create" or a delight in plastic form or color as such. This overpowering faith is the lifeblood of great art. It is one of the qualities that distinguish great art from that craftsmanship which, however competent, is just good painting.

Rousseau saw the world through the eyes of a wide-eyed child. To most adults, an event, scene, vista or whatnot arouses its set responses. These responses will vary from person to person but are generally explicable—translatable into words, forms, colors, perhaps even into music for the piano. To Rousseau, however, life was ever a new experience, mysterious and inexplicable. Beneath the look of things, he felt, lay an inner and arcane essence. Life to him remained an eternal riddle, and the mystical note in his pictures bears witness to the depth of his awe and the breadth of his emotional feeling.

He painted a great many scenes in and about Paris: streets, squares, bridges, the Eiffel Tower and the Trocadéro, the Parc Montsouris, the Buttes Chaumont, the fortifications, Malakoff, villages along the Seine and the Oise. None of these pictures is of particular interest as a documentary record. But all are fascinating imaginative records, in a curious and intensely personal way far surpassing strict documentation. The view of the Eiffel Tower and the Trocadéro as seen through the trees from a bridge over the Seine, for example, is hardly "documentary" in any degree. Yet it is much more; it is a picture of spring, of evening, of youthful desires, of nightingales hidden in the trees and unheard melodies rising from river and bridge.

Or again: on rainy days, heavy clouds like these doubtless hover over Malakoff and Gentilly. But note: they are not mere clouds; they are the shifting curtains behind which awestruck children try to peer when waiting for a glimpse of God hurling down His thunderbolts from heaven. Still again: here is a road on the outskirts of a country town. It has been carefully planted with trees and shrubs which half-hide the barren fields beyond it. Who did not, as a child living in the country, dawdle along this road when taking Sunday walks with the family? How slowly the time dragged by! How dreary life seemed, as we danced along impatiently before our plodding parents! The trees and shrubs mask the dullness of the countryside no better than those Sunday walks masked the monotonies of our existence.

Rousseau knew next to nothing of the fashionable, worldly Paris—the glittering Paris of impeccable public gardens, stately public buildings and the magnificent Champs Elysées. His was a depressed and depressing city of back streets and barrack-like houses. His affection for it partook of the resigned melancholy of the place itself. His pictures of its streets and scenes are wordless essays on the endurance of the human spirit.

But now and again, this Paris became too depressing for even him to endure, and he withdrew to a lush dream-world of tropical jungle.

Then he would alter the very scale of his work, replacing a small-sized canvas with one that all but filled his little room.

It is a veritable dream-world, out of no garden, zoo or cinema studio, but straight from the fearsome and beautiful shadows of childhood fantasy. Palm groves glisten in the moonlight along a broad river. Lions peer from tall canebrakes; gay-colored birds perch motionless amid preternaturally large leaves; apes swing from treetop to treetop. In the night the scream of a black man struck down by a panther is heard, or the flute of a black woman luring snakes from their holes. The story goes that while painting these jungle scenes, Rousseau was sometimes so fevered by his conception that he would break off work and throw open a window for air. His huge landscape called "The Dream" is a climactic blend of the charms, horrors, dangers and delights of his imagination—with Yadwigha lying calmly in the midst of it all on a red sofa. The secret of the picture's power is not the striking color contrast (red sofa *vs.* jungle green), but the extraordinary evocation of a mysterious and incredible world. Rousseau finished it off with a verbal postscript:

> *Yadwigha dans un beau rêve*
> *S'étant endormie doucement*
> *Entendait les sons d'une musette*
> *Dont jouait un charmeur bien pensant.*
> *Pendante que la lune reflète*
> *Sur les fleurs, les arbres verdoyants,*
> *Les fauves serpents prêtent l'oreille*
> *Aux airs gayes de l'instrument.**

Rousseau's portraits are among his most important works, even though he understood little of the infinite variety of human behavior. To him, all men were brothers, as Jesus had preached, and he tried his best to say so in his portraits. But within this limit of his capacity, he showed remarkable analytical powers. His first thought was to find settings

---

* Yadwigha lay sleeping sweetly
Wrapped in a blissful dream,
While the liquid notes of a piper
Pervaded the jungle scene.
The moonlight shines down brightly
On lush jungle flowers and leaves,
And the lurking serpents listen
To the gay tune the music weaves.

(*Tr.*)

HENRI ROUSSEAU: THE PROMENADE

HENRI ROUSSEAU: SUMMER; THE PASTURE (THE LOUVRE MUSEUM, PARIS)

that would convey what he felt to be the personality of his subjects—not merely those backgrounds which would best accentuate the chosen flesh tones. He posed his beloved young wife, for example, in a flower garden beneath a peaceful, cloud-flecked sky. In all art there are few portraits more eloquent than this. Spring-like odors seem to rise from it, quite as the *Nike* of Samothrace seems redolent of ocean spray. It is more than portraiture; it is a hymn to youth and love. *6445*

In another picture, a young woman stands in a leafing grove, the pink of sunset gleaming through the trees. She has stopped in the course of a promenade and lifted her hand to her heart, as though overcome by the surrounding scene—a most beautiful statement of the hopes and emotions of young womanhood. There is also a pair of small portraits of Rousseau and his wife when they were no longer young. The faces stand out from a severe background, but an oil lamp placed boldly in each portrait suggests domestic peace and harmony as no conventionally cluttered interior would have been likely to do.

Particularly noteworthy is a large self-portrait. Rousseau stands proud and solemn, palette in hand, on a quai across the Seine from the Louvre. The names of his two wives are written on the palette: *Clémence et Joséphine*. Nearby lies a ship hung with gay pennants and flags. How better could he have testified to his devotion, his self-dedication, his love and his pride? This remarkable painting is a more telling analysis of his life and work than anything a critic could set down on the printed page.

Occasionally he sensed and was able to reproduce peculiar states of mind, as in his portrait (owned by Picasso) of a woman standing on a curtained balcony and holding an inverted leafy bough as though it were a cane. The pose, as well as the bizarre landscape seen through the railing of the balcony, suggests most clearly a neurotic personality. In portraiture as in the rest of his work, Rousseau's imagination sought out latent significances. He posed a child in a meadow sprinkled with tiny blossoms and put a daisy in its hand; but the poet Guillaume Apollinaire is posed behind a row of gaudy, upstanding flowers.

It has been charged that Rousseau's portraits are wretched likenesses. His friend Alfred Jarry is reported to have said that when he came to sit for Rousseau, the artist measured off his nose, mouth, ears, etc., on the handle of his brush, and then reproduced the measurements exactly, without due allowance for perspective. He is also said to have held his paints close to the sitter's face, in order to determine the proper flesh tones. Certainly Rousseau had a number of odd and highly original ways of painting. But if here and there his portraits seem to be poor resemblances, it should be remembered that he was trying to capture what he saw as the personality, and hence was interested in features only as they reflected the heart and mind.

Rousseau's sense of form was as highly developed as his sense of fantasy. His work is craftsmanlike as well as creative, his drawing clean and sure. Plants and trees all but live and grow on his canvasses; like Corot, he had the great gift of infusing them with reality, branch by branch, leaf by leaf, flower by flower.

His composition is a triumph of space perception, delicately plotted and sensitively balanced. An almost palpable rhythm flows through the "View of Gentilly," formerly owned by Charles Guérin. What could be more appropriate to the theme than the simple harmonies of design in the portrait of the child with the dangling puppet? In the portrait owned by Picasso, how deftly the various bizarre details are oriented and interrelated by the single detail of the bird in the upper corner! How cleverly placed is the woman in "The Promenade" so as to serve as a focal point for the entire grove! Some of Rousseau's jungle landscapes have a fundamental symmetry found elsewhere only in the work of Poussin. His work in this respect is altogether within the great tradition of French painting.

His sense of color values was no less notable. The blues, violets and pinks are both subtle and beautiful, the greens and blacks simply incomparable. Certain of his pictures are done almost entirely in a gamut of greens, and his bold use of black astonished Gauguin and has left lesser painters gasping. "Matisse's pinks and light greens," I noted in *Picasso et la Tradition Française*, "are artful and tasteful, Manet's brown is brilliantly effective, but Rousseau's black grips the very soul." I went on to compare it to the deep note of a tolling cathedral bell, and Matisse's pinks to the gaiety of a breakfast gong. Rousseau had no theory of color, but fully understood its possibilities and became an absolute master of its effects. The gloomy gray-greens in his view of the Paris fortifications accent precisely the cheerless remoteness of the spot. The pinks, grays and light greens of his "Snake Charmer," on the other hand, are

36

HENRI ROUSSEAU: THE WATERFALL

(COLLECTION OF THE ART INSTITUTE OF CHICAGO, HELEN BIRCH BARTLETT MEMORIAL)

so seductive that one can almost hear the notes of the snake charmer's flute.

Yet colors, like patterns and forms, were but a means to an end. Translating them to their simplest and most significant terms, Rousseau used them to express what his heart impelled him to say. He studied literal detail, often making drawings in the Jardin des Plantes, or going out in autumn to gather leaves and grasses for examination at home. Much as Pissarro and Sisley had done, he drew sketches from life for certain of his landscapes, among them those of the fortifications, the Eiffel Tower and the Parc Montsouris. He was a conscious stylist, interpreting color, form and pattern in his own way.

When I first met him (through the mother of my friend Robert Delaunay) he was working on "The Snake Charmer," which now hangs in the Louvre. It did not take me long to realize how passionately he devoted himself to the task of mastering the teeming visions of his brain. Yet as long as he lived, there were critics who could see nothing in his work but naiveté and inanity. These worthies never missed a chance, at the annual Independent shows or the *Salons d'Automne*, to display their own naiveté and inanity by poking cheap fun at Henri Rousseau.

★　　　★

About two years before his death, the Douanier had his first one-man show. A furniture dealer in the Faubourg St. Antoine asked me to hang a few pictures in a room on the Rue Notre Dame des Champs where he was exhibiting his tables and chairs. My first thought was of Rousseau. He himself brought over a number of his works in a pushcart, and we hung them together. I sent out the invitations, but forgot to include the address of our little "gallery," so only a few visitors appeared. I bought the delightful "Malakoff" at the show for 40 francs—about twice what it would have commanded in the open market. His work in general had very little value in those days. He did a large and admirable portrait of an American art dealer named Brummer, who had a prosperous shop on the Boulevard Raspail; and Brummer himself offered me this for 35 francs.

After the Douanier's death there was not enough money to meet his funeral expenses, so the unsold pictures in his room were auctioned off among his friends. The painter Férat bought the now-famous "Wedding" for 200 francs, and I bought the portrait of Rousseau's first wife for the same price. Several years later the pictures had still not increased in value. Even the publication of my little *Henri Rousseau* a year after the artist's death did not greatly alter matters in this respect, although the interest accorded the book and the speed with which the edition was bought up indicated that his work was beginning to be understood. Félix Fénéon, then in charge of the modern section of the Bernheim Jeune Gallery, agreed at my urging to a full-fledged retrospective show, but the consent of the Messrs. Bernheim was more difficult to obtain. The exhibit opened at last on October 28, 1912.

For months prior to that date, I spent considerable time trying to locate unknown Rousseaus, visiting people in and about the Plaisance quarter who I knew had been acquainted with the Douanier, and in some streets going from house to house making random inquiries of the concierges. One of my discoveries was in the flat of one of Rousseau's lady friends, a laundress who lived in the Impasse du Maine. There, standing before the fireplace, covered with soot (it had been used as a firescreen), was the charming early picture of a young woman in red walking in a spring wood. The laundress was willing to sell, but could scarcely bring herself to name the price, for she considered it outrageously high: 40 francs.

She added that some relatives of hers, farmers living near Amiens, had other early pictures. I went to see these people, driving out from Amiens in a rain so heavy that I bogged down several times in the mud. They, it developed, had four Rousseaus, but the farmer wasn't at home, and his wife said that she had become too attached to the pictures to think of selling them. Later the farmer wrote a friendly letter inviting me to call and have a chat about Rousseau and a couple of drinks as well. I was bedridden with rheumatism contracted during the moist adventure just concluded, so I had to decline, but eventually managed to buy the pictures anyhow. Nor did I forget to visit Rousseau's daughter. She had married a traveling salesman and was living in Angers. I found, though, that she had only one small picture. The others, I was informed, had "luckily" been destroyed.

HENRI ROUSSEAU: THE SLEEPING GYPSY (THE MUSEUM OF MODERN ART, NEW YORK)

HENRI ROUSSEAU: THE SNAKE CHARMER (THE LOUVRE MUSEUM, PARIS)

I prepared a preface for the catalogue of the Bernheim Jeune exhibit. The exhibit itself was successful in that it brought Rousseau's work to the notice of a number of influential people. Important collectors began to show signs of interest, among them Alphonse Kann in Paris and Edwin Suermondt and Paul von Mendelssohn-Bartholdy in Germany. Encouraged by this, I ventured to exhibit a number of the pictures in Germany—as a reward for which, of course, the press heaped mockery upon my head.

Soon, however, the auction of an English collection showed how the tide was turning. Among works by Degas, Van Gogh, Gauguin and Cézanne were two small sketches and a large jungle scene by Rousseau. The sketches brought 1000 francs each, the jungle scene 9000. Rousseau's portrait of Pierre Loti was put on display in the window of the Rosenberg Gallery on the Avenue de l'Opéra—priced, as I remember it, at 6000 francs. This portrait had been the property of Courteline, popular author of light comedies, who had hung it in his renowned "Chamber of Horrors." Courteline simply could not understand why a painting he had always considered a joke should now be worth so large a sum.

Yet the scornful public laughter was by no means stilled. It rang through the cloister on the Boulevard des Invalides as long as I lived there, a tenant of the State, and it followed when I moved myself and my collection to the quai opposite the Ile St. Louis. Twice each week, on visiting days, it echoed through my rooms, then down the staircase, into the vestibule and out upon the street—inspired partly by the works of Picasso and Braque, which also hung on my walls, but above all by those of Rousseau.

Nevertheless, one morning brought the proof of impending fame: forgeries. A young man appeared at my place with two canvases under his arm, one a picture of a tiger. He explained that these were the work of the great Henri Rousseau, and suggested that I buy them. A single glance sufficed to show that they were bad imitations. I said nothing, but set the pictures next to a genuine work and with a smile and wave of the hand invited comparison. About a week thereafter, when I visited a dealer whose brother later became a Rousseau specialist, he proudly displayed both forgeries as his newest acquisitions. In later years I often saw them in other places.

Then came an experience I shall never forget. On the last day of July, 1914, friends helped me dress and led me downstairs to a carriage. With war inevitable, I had become an enemy alien and had to return to Germany. Since I could move only at a walk—for weeks I had had typhoid fever without realizing it, and had run an almost continuous fever of 104°—I had time as I dressed to bid farewell to each of my pictures. There was the portrait of Brummer in his black suit. There was the little girl with a doll in one hand, a daisy in the other. There was the red lady in the spring wood, and "Malakoff," and "The Promenade." . . . Each of these pictures had, for me, its own history, and each had become part of my life.

The relationship was indestructible. Wartime sequestration and sale of my collection severed only the outward ties. Some ten years later, on the day I returned to my beloved Paris, I was sitting in a cafe on one of the main boulevards. As I looked around, I suddenly saw the name of Henri Rousseau in large type. It was printed on a poster advertising an exhibit of modern art in a neighboring department store, the Maison de Blanc. I went there immediately, and was recognized by an amiable gentleman wearing the rosette of the Legion of Honor. He asked which of the pictures I had been most fond of. Deeply stirred by old memories, I walked from one to another, and finally stopped before the red lady in a spring wood. "That's for sale," said the gentleman, softly. "I'll never be able to buy it again," I replied. "The asking price is 300,000 francs," the gentleman added; "times have changed."

Times indeed had changed. Dealers and collectors alike, excited by the publication of high-priced monographs, were falling over one another to buy Rousseaus. Genuine examples soon vanished from the market, and the inevitable frauds took their place. A German dealer met me on the street one day. "Ah, you're back!" he observed dryly; "I suppose you've already dug up some new Rousseaus." I told him that I hadn't tried to. "Yesterday," he went on, "I was lucky enough to find three for the ridiculous price of 50,000 francs. What do you say to that?"

I said that he had done well if they were genuine, but not so well if they were fakes, and asked him to describe the pictures. When he did so, I explained that I knew them and that they were patent fakes. "Good God," he cried, "what shall I do? I used a customer's money in the deal, and I'm responsible." "Well," I said, "return the pictures to whoever

44

sold them to you and ask for your money back. Say it was I who told you they were fakes."

The following day I met the dealer again. He was wreathed in smiles. "That chap is an angel. Naturally he didn't want to take the pictures back, but he made me a present of a wonderful Rousseau portrait to seal the bargain. 'Even your friend won't try to make out that this is bogus,' he told me. The portrait alone is worth more than 50,000 francs." As might be expected, it wasn't. The portrait was a forgery, too.

It so happened that I still owned a Rousseau sketch—a very small but excellent work. I made up my mind to sell it, for it was the one valuable object I had left, and I needed the money to start life again in Paris. Someone told me of a dealer who had recently begun to specialize in Rousseau. I had known him before the war, for as a young man he had tried to sell me some Negro sculptures, and I had once visited his attic on the Rue des Martyrs. Now when I called he was living in a sumptuous apartment in an elegant part of the city—and, incidentally, had the first Modiglianis and Soutines I ever saw. He took my little Rousseau to show to his wife. In a few minutes he came back to tell me that it wasn't important enough for him to bother with.

Years later I visited him again, to ask him to lend me Rousseau's "Wedding" for an exhibit. By then he had moved to a still larger place in a still more fashionable quarter. At the top of an immense stairway stood a maître d'hôtel in formal clothes, with a heavy gold chain around his neck. This dignitary escorted me into a room one whole wall of which was covered with Rousseaus. "Well, I've never lent the 'Wedding' to anybody," said its owner, "but I can hardly refuse you. There's one qualification, though: you'll have to pay the insurance premium, and that's high, for the picture set me back about 1,000,000 francs." I could not help thinking sadly of the old days when a few hundred francs had been high for any Rousseau; and when, by foregoing other things I needed or wanted, I could buy their incomparable beauty and have it for my own.

In the interval "The Snake Charmer" had been bought from the elder Mme. Delaunay by the famous collector Doucet; and Doucet, in turn, had bequeathed it to the Louvre. One day a friend rushed up to me on the street and cried, "Have you heard the news? The 'Charmer' has just been hung!" Tremendously excited, I jumped into a taxi and hastened to the Louvre. Unfortunately, the gallery with the Corots, Manets, Degases, etc., was not open. A watchman told me that part of the roof had fallen and that it would take several weeks to repair the damage. But he confirmed the great news I had heard, adding that a picture by Manet had been rehung to make room for the picture by Rousseau.

The moment finally came when I saw it hanging on the wall in all its splendor. I thought of the little Douanier, now ranked a master among masters. I thought too of the time when he and I were probably the only people on earth who considered this even a remote possibility.

Not many years later the Louvre was closed and its pictures hidden away. Once again war impended. When this war too was won and France was again free, it so happened that there were few qualified Rousseau experts on hand. Perhaps it was assumed that they had died or otherwise vanished forever; in any event, there was issued in Paris a Rousseau study illustrated with upward of 25 forgeries. And Maximilien Gauthier identified about half the pictures at a certain Rousseau show as downright frauds.

A genuine work of prime quality, however, long considered lost, turned up during this period. Entitled "War," it too was acquired by the Louvre. A half century earlier—in 1894—Rousseau had foreseen, through the magical medium of great art, the horrors experienced by humanity during recent years.

HENRI ROUSSEAU: THE DREAM OF YADWIGHA (COLLECTION SIDNEY JANIS, NEW YORK)

LOUIS VIVIN: THE MARSH

L O U I S   V I V I N

The grandeur and gaiety of Paris lie close to its heart. Notre Dame, the Louvre and its pictures, the plashing fountains of the Tuileries, the spacious magnificence of the Place de la Concorde, the matchless Avenue des Champs Elysées and its ultimate Arc de Triomphe—all these abut or adjoin the great artery of the city, the Seine. And when night falls, there is laughter, music and dancing on either side of the river in Montmartre and Montparnasse, twin pleasure zones.

But remote from this heart, fanning out toward the fortifications, is another and duller Paris—the Paris of mean streets, obscure lives, dingy and crowded homes. Louis Vivin lived in one such street behind Montmartre, in a section as prosaic as any provincial town.

His house, like most of the others roundabout, was old, weatherstained and rundown. Up a narrow stairway lay its flats, each identical (two rooms and kitchen) and each inhabited by some petty clerk or pensioner. The place was neither bourgeois nor proletarian. No house-to-house salesmen bothered to peddle their wares here of a morning and no well-dressed ladies sauntered out for tea in the afternoon. There were not even stout, perspiring mothers lugging laundry pails around, or children playing noisy games upon the stairs. As a rule, the house was as deserted as a tomb, every footstep resounding hollowly through uncarpeted halls. Forlorn-faced women went out to do their shopping early. Their grim-faced men hurried home for lunch and hurried back as quickly to their jobs. Then the halls were all but empty until evening.

Vivin's flat was on the fifth floor. His visitors had to climb past eight other flats on the way up, one distinguished from its neighbor only by a milkcan instead of a breadbag hanging from the doorknob, or an electric pushbutton instead of an old-style bellpull. Vivin and the tenant across the hall each had a "terrace"—*i.e.*, a tiny balcony with space for a single person or a single chair. There was that advantage, at least, to living on the fifth floor. Vivin would be standing on his balcony whenever I came to call, and would wait there to wave goodbye as I reached the street on the way home. He was a tall man, bent with age. His features were thin and intense. He wore an old-fashioned beard and let his wispy gray hair grow long.

His easel stood in the one well-lighted part of the room, close to the balcony window. On the table and chairs roundabout lay piles of illustrated books, magazines, loose flower prints, chromolithographed picture postcards. These illustrations were Vivin's models; here was a universe embalmed and on file. As the spirit moved him, he chose one item or another from the file, set it up before him, and brought it to life and gave it stature by the sheer force of his artistic imagination.

Day after day he followed a fixed schedule. At five a.m. he rose, lit a kerosene lamp and took up brushes and mahlstick. He always used a mahlstick, for the details of his work required a steady hand and precise care. He would break off only for meals or for a regular afternoon walk through the streets of the neighborhood.

He rarely varied his route, and never visited art galleries except when he himself had pictures on display. Then he might drop in to note the public reaction. At an exhibit I arranged in the Quatre Chemins Gallery, the first visitor happened to be one of his warmest admirers, Diaghileff. Diaghileff immediately went up to the old man and introduced himself. "Are you," Vivin inquired, "a painter too?" Diaghileff, amused that there should be anyone who didn't recognize his name, struck an odd little pose and replied, "*Ah non, je danse plutôt*"—"Somehow I dance." Vivin knew nothing of such exotic, nightblooming careers. He was invariably in bed before nine p.m., leaving his devoted wife to sit up alone with the sorrows that usually beset two old people restricted by circumstance and two small rooms.

★　　★

Vivin's life was always restricted, even in the days when he worked for the French postal service. True, he was in the mobile branch, and thus

LOUIS VIVIN: CHURCH INTERIOR

traveled about the country a good deal, but always in a windowless railway mail car, lighted from above and walled by tiers of pigeonholes. The chief result of his travels was a series of maps of the postal districts in France, in which he showed the exact location of each postoffice, and thereby won two years' seniority and ultimately the rank of inspector and the ribbon of the *Palmes Académiques*. This sequence of events, the one break in a life of routine, was but a limited triumph. The maps over which he worked so hard were never published. The postal authorities concluded that the cost of printing would be too high.

When I met Vivin, he had retired on a pension and was painting from dawn till dark. He was born at Hadol, in the Vosges, in 1861. As a boy he ornamented the doors of the family homestead, and, at 20-odd, painted a series of landscapes of Hadol and vicinity. Later he moved to Paris, and while there went to visit the galleries of the Luxembourg and the Louvre. The old masters left him unimpressed, but he liked Corot and Courbet, and fell in love with Meissonnier. One night he had a vision: Meissonnier appeared in a dream and told him that he could be a great artist if he tried.

What appealed to Vivin was Meissonnier's taste for detail, and he cultivated the same taste in his own work. His pictures of Paris, based largely on literal illustration, are built up of minute and literal detail, brick by brick and stone by stone, just as his career in the postal service and later in retirement was composed of routines unvarying from day to day.

Yet Vivin's pictures are by no means mere documents, reproducing scenes and events with whatever factual accuracy he could muster. He could never have endured a life of severe routine, doggedly following a set schedule in a gloomy room, had he been interested simply in "accuracy" or "realism." He was no pedantic, realistic reporter. On the contrary, he was a pathologically bitter critic, to whom a career of drab monotony seemed as ineluctable as salt water to a fish in the sea.

★　　★

This bitterness dominates his work and subdues all elements of conventional "reality." His work is, indeed, the expression of a wholly unconventional state of mind, verging at points on the hysteric. Vivin's canvases may seem "realistic"; every brick and stone, every feature and object, may bespeak a literal intention. But beneath the apparently reportorial surface is a savage sense of tragedy. Louis Vivin was in no respect the Canaletto of modern Paris.

This sense of tragedy lay unfathomably deep. It was inherent in his nature, a kind of doom. It colored his views of the processes of life, not merely his attitude toward himself or toward man in general. Consider the themes he often chose: ships wrecked in storms, animals tearing one another to bits or waylaid and slaughtered by hunters. I know of no paintings more painfully tragic than, say, his picture of a child lost through the ice or that of a woman broken with anguish as a coffin is borne from her home. No poem by Baudelaire is as bitter as Vivin's picture of the Belfort war memorial. Done in dark grays and blues, it suggests an eternity of cold, clammy November days, as though for years rain had fallen like tears on the little public square, and at any moment would start falling again.

The tragic note is latent even in ostensibly cheerful scenes. What could be gayer at first glance than the noisy reds and greens of his picture of the Père Frédéric cabaret? But observe the grim lodging houses adjacent. They seem to represent the lasting truth of the scene; the cabaret is something here today, gone tomorrow. What could be gayer than the merry-go-rounds and side-shows in his picture called "The Fair"? But again observe the environment: dirty gray pavements, factory-like tenements, dingy red-brick walls.

There is, Vivin seems to say, no true relation between life's pleasures, all too soon ended, and the desperate normality which endures. Here is a view of a frozen pond, with a few naked willows in the background and a small pavilion almost certainly icy and empty inside. A number of people are skating on the pond, and there is a welcome little booth for warm refreshments. But the sun has set. Night and cold seem to be waiting impatiently to overwhelm the scene. Sadness is normal, eternal, endless. Joy is but lent and soon withdrawn.

It is almost as though Vivin's "realistic" landscapes were deliberate fronts or façades for other landscapes behind. A millwheel clacks merrily away at the edge of a stream, but the mill itself seems set there to hide the desolate countryside beyond. A village church steeple rises guardian-like

LOUIS VIVIN: VENICE

LOUIS VIVIN: THE FAIR

above a cluster of houses, but what of the threatening snow clouds hanging low over the surrounding plain? There are terrifying vistas in Vivin: roads one dare not follow, houses one dare not leave, hedges over which one dare not peer. Tragedy lurks in the middle distance, and beyond the horizon lies despair.

But not always. Now and then a note of genuine pleasure shows in his work, quite as now and then when we were talking together his somber countenance would break into a cheerful smile. The flowers and fruits in his still-lifes are the free gift of bounteous nature; some of his landscapes are bathed in that air of soft contentment found in Corot. When so disposed, he drew scenes as peaceful and delightful as the miniatures of Fouquet, or pastorals as charmingly detailed as the illumination by the brothers Limbourg in the Duc de Berry's *Book of Hours*. Done in the same spirit are his pictures of rural weddings and dances, of boat trips, picnics, horseraces, winter sports, animals in zoos, pious folk at church, swans drifting on an unruffled pond. As a young man, he painted scenes of family groups sitting placidly around a table, or handicrafters busy at their work. There are even a few of obviously waggish or roguish intent.

It follows that Vivin was an artist gripped by the deepest feelings, torn by diverse and powerful emotions. Occasionally his acute awareness of human solitude, his compassion for the sorrows of man and beast, gave way before his pleasure in a sunlit prospect or the manifold delights of an Ile de France garden. As a rule, the skies in his pictures press heavily upon the earth, ready to strike with lightning, flood with rain, blast with hail, or simply to darken and sicken the hearts of men. But now and again fleecy clouds drift peacefully through his skies, like sheep through a meadow, and sometimes his heavens shine in a gentle and cloudless blue.

★ ★

Vivin might be called an early Surrealist because of the mystic and gruesome in his work—the sense there of a supernatural fourth dimension. (It may be noted in passing that for a time he was interested in spiritualistic or psychic phenomena.) Surrealism in painting, however, is essentially a movement of studied or "literary" effects. The depths of Vivin's feelings as well as qualities of his work serve to distinguish him from the movement as such.

He had many strong and individual qualities. He was by no means merely the emotionalist. People who knew no better used to dismiss him as a minor master of static and more or less unvarying architectural views, but by now the scope of his work should be clear to any careful observer. He had a remarkable eye for color, and achieved bold and startling effects: deep blue in a belfry, gleaming red in the tongue of a stag, delicate pink in the Place de la Concorde obelisk, violent yellow in the Dôme des Invalides cupola or the sail of a ship. His sea-greens, the duns and tans used for old woodwork or wild animals, the blues used for skies or windowpanes—these have the matchless beauty of precious stones, flowers, butterfly wings. His coastal scenes—of Royan and, notably, of Venice—borrow the choicest and freshest colors of nature and blend them into a harmonious whole.

Extraordinary above all are his grays. A superb dark range is employed in the early Notre Dame pictures, likewise in those of the Place du Tertre, the Montmartre mills and people playing at bowls. In other pictures these dark grays are used for wild boar, or for a cliff against which a ship is wrecked, or for ominous winter skies—and generally in heavy, handsome textures reminiscent of Courbet. Vivin's work is also rich in yellow grays and blue grays, with a great deal of clean, gleaming light gray in his snow scenes and architectural views.

The dark and the light are occasionally juxtaposed—e.g., when dogs and wild boar are silhouetted against the snow, or when a shirt is contrasted with a waistcoat in a portrait. Or occasionally these grays, light and dark, are juxtaposed uncompromisingly with yellows, greens or blues, greatly increasing the tonal qualities of each in the process. Here there is no harmony whatsoever, but counterpoint of striking beauty. Vivin thus made use of the color harmonies which gave Delacroix his power, the gray tones which Le Nain, Chardin and Corot used to perfection, and the color counterpoint of which Manet was the great master. His work both derives from and dovetails into the traditions of French art.

He painted what he felt as well as what he saw—significance as well as surface. Thus he arrived at results resembling those Picassos in which the several parts of a figure or object are distorted to produce an effective *supra-verum*. In sketching Notre Dame, for example, Vivin set side-elevation and front-elevation cheek by jowl. His zoological gardens swarm with animals that would never be found together in real life. His Notre Dame and his zoo alike rise far above the literal or photographic in sheer intensity.

Furthermore, spatial relationships are of no more over-riding importance in Vivin than in Picasso. The object to be pictured—man, building, tree, etc.—was itself what interested him, not the logic with which it seemed to fit into one or another set of surroundings. In most of Vivin, depth and perspective are handled normally enough, but now and then he drew his background figures larger than those in the foreground— e.g., when there happened to be architectural details in the background that he wanted to stress. The effect is often similar to that of certain pictures by Italian Primitives.

The spirit in which Vivin worked made it inevitable that he should stress compositional rather than spatial relationships. It was his marked sense of rhythm, balance and compositional design, rather than the reportorial "facts" of a given case, that dictated the distribution of details in his pictures—the grouping of items in a still-life, or the arrangement of ships at anchor in harbor, people walking a street, animals coursing a landscape.

He was an artist of spontaneous perceptions and natural gifts, yet as time went on his work increased in power, as a great artist's will. This evolution may be clearly traced. To begin with, there are his youthful views of household interiors, kittens at play, parks, etc.; then come tensely emotional seascapes and landscapes and such bitterly tragic pictures as "The Stag and the Wolves." Vivin's earlier work in general is active in mood and narrative in purpose, even the indicated environment expressing the flux of pressures he saw in life as a whole. But, bit by bit in his later work, the active mood vanishes. Ducks no longer paddle the ponds. Streets are emptied of pedestrians and vehicles. At last there is no longer even the play of light across an architectural façade.

Vivin's final pictures are almost abstract, his interest in architecture reducing itself to interest in blocks of color and form, his pervasive artistry assuming complete control of his emotions. Freed of preoccupation with detail, concentrated on essential meanings alone, his work achieves a massive simplicity of effect and something of that tactile, tangible directness Berenson noted in Giotto. At the outset simply conceptual and local in connotation, Vivin's art gradually approached the palpable and universal. Like Picasso and Braque in their "heroic periods," he became more and more intent upon tactile values, and in fact produced actual surface relief in a number of his pictures by the application of plaster. As his own physical horizon grew narrower and dimmer, he lightened and brightened the tonalities of his painting.

Henri Rousseau, the Douanier, fabricated a fabulous dream world in his little chamber on the Rue Perrel. In a little bedroom in Senlis (as we shall see), an aging housemaid named Séraphine created still another world, religious and psychotic rather than fabulous in cast. And in a little flat behind Montmartre, Louis Vivin, ex-postal clerk, created still a third —an immeasurable world, extending from the depth of his secret grief up toward the exaltations of Fra Angelico, and from the utterly familiar and workaday centers of life out toward the remote fringes of abstraction.

Whenever I think of Vivin, I think of a character in a Maeterlinck play. He is an old man sitting quietly in a lamplit room. Suddenly he becomes aware of inexorable powers surrounding him and his household; and then, without quite realizing it, he correctly interprets the meaning of a strange silence out of doors and the oil-lamp's sibilance within the room. Humbled and baffled by the experience, he bows his head, never suspecting that the basic forces of life itself have been his prompters and tutors. I believe, as apparently Maeterlinck does, that a man of this sort, old or not, more nearly lives life to its emotional full than the most passionate lover or the greatest general flushed with victory in the field.

★ ★

I first met Vivin in 1925, visiting his flat after seeing some of his pictures in an inconspicuous Montmartre gallery. By then he had been retired from the postal service for two or three years. During my first call, he showed me the pictures he had been painting in the interval, as well as a number of early works—one of his birthplace in Hadol, with a large linden tree in the dooryard, and smaller views of the village itself, generally showing the church steeple. Hanging on one wall of his flat, practically hidden by the accumulation of prints and illustrated volumes

LOUIS VIVIN: STILL LIFE

L. VIVIN

LOUIS VIVIN: THE DROWNED MISTRESS

which filled the room, was a very large marsh scene with a solitary heron. Vivin had painted this in 1889, and had shown it at an exhibit of work done by employees of the postal service. I took it to the courtyard of the Latin Quarter hotel in which I was then living and washed away the accumulated dust of thirty-five years.

After that first visit, I spent hour after hour with the old man, silently studying his pictures as he worked away at his easel. Occasionally I could not resist exclaiming over something particularly fine, or suggesting changes in details that seemed less effective than they might be. Vivin never took my advice. "It has to be that way," he would earnestly explain, and there the matter ended.

In this respect he was quite different from Rousseau or Séraphine. The former was working on "The Snake Charmer" when we met, and would often ask me whether, for the sake of balance and harmony, this or that detail should be darker or lighter. Now and then Séraphine would ask similar questions. At that point, their inspiration, or vision—in which, of course, no one else could share—was complete, and they were interested in translating it to canvas in the most effective way possible.

With Vivin, though, the two processes were as one. With him, execution was also intuitive, and no outside advice could be entertained. I am now convinced that the old man was almost always right. Certain pictures that appeared to have obvious shortcomings when I first saw them now strike me as among his best. It has been my experience that Vivin's work may be slow to communicate, and that the wise man will wait in patience until the moment comes.

★　　　★

Toward the close of his life, Vivin was no longer able to paint. I called one day to find that he had had a stroke. His right arm and speech were paralyzed. He recovered somewhat, only to suffer another stroke. Remaining as calm and cordial as ever, he would still go to his balcony to watch until I disappeared from sight, but he could no longer wave goodbye. Most of his waking hours were spent sitting by the window and reading the books I brought to keep him entertained.

But he had never had, and had never needed, much worldly entertainment. The delights of Paris, which the whole world knows, had never been his. Using every ounce of strength and talent, he had shaped a world of his own, and that was now complete. The sixth day had passed. On the seventh he rested, God having granted him the peace and clarity to survey his work.

Louis Vivin died on May 28, 1936, aged seventy-five. The funeral service in the little church of Ste. Geneviève des Grandes Carrières was attended by relatives, a few neighborhood friends, and my sister and me. He was buried in the Pantin cemetery.

He died poor and obscure, but his work is an enduring legacy, *aere perennius*. His widow soon followed him, and the shabby little flat I knew so well was transformed almost overnight. Its bourgeois banality returned; its mysterious aura vanished. Out went the hoarded stacks of picture books and bound magazines, the worn tables and the easel, the bedstead so lovingly painted with clouds and hovering angels. The two rooms and kitchen were swept, cleaned, painted and polished. New tenants lugged garish new furniture up those steep flights of stairs. Soon every trace of the presence of genius disappeared.

But not the proof thereof. Vivin's work is secure forever in the history of art and the hearts of men.

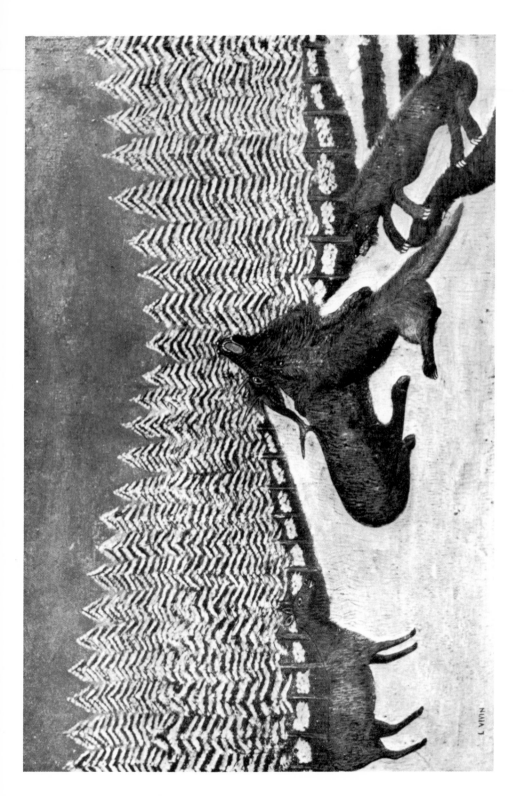

LOUIS VIVIN: THE STAG AND THE WOLVES

LOUIS VIVIN: THE DOME DES INVALIDES

ANDRE BAUCHANT

It must have been in 1925, about a year after I resettled in Paris, that I left the current *Salon d'Automne* in a depressed mood. By and large, the show had been a disappointment. Only one thing had appealed to me at all—a picture of some wolves in a snowy forest. On the way out, I ran into a friend. We were discussing how bad the show had been when it developed that he too had been impressed by that one picture. André Bauchant was the artist's name.

I don't now recall whether I heard or saw anything more of Bauchant's work during the next year or so. But in 1927 I went to a show put on by Madame Jeanne Bucher, and there discovered that he had already won a number of admirers, and that Le Corbusier and Ozenfant, among others, had been collecting him for several years. Madame Bucher took me in hand and introduced me to the artist. He was a tall, lean man with a pointed beard. He wore the sort of ill-fitting suit that peasants wear to weddings and funerals, and was clearly not at ease among the throng of city folk and strangers.

I learned more about Bauchant when Madame Bucher gave me a copy of a letter that he himself had written to Maurice Raynal. He was born in Château-Renault, near Tours, on April 24, 1873. At the age of fifteen he left the village school and went to work as a farm hand, then served his term in the French Army. Somehow he became interested in literature and history. He read what he could of the classics, and later, when traveling on business through central and western France, visited historical sites and cities—also art museums, although he had little or no background in art. Called to the colors during the first World War, he served as a bookkeeper and then as a telemetric draftsman in Rheims, and made a series of panoramic sketches of the Battle of the Marne which were exhibited in the 1921 *Salon d'Automne*.

The letter to Raynal, written in 1922, alludes to the following pictures, which thus may be dated 1922 or earlier: "Pericles Accounting for His Use of Public Monies," "The Battle of Thermopylae," "The Proclamation of American Independence," "Washington Reading the Proclamation in the Presence of Rochambeau and Lafayette," "The Battle of Palermo in the Punic Wars" (with elephants), "The Expulsion of Adam and Eve from Paradise," and "The Rescue of Andromeda by Perseus."*

Evidently Bauchant's interest in historical subjects had lessened by 1927. At any rate, I remember particularly in his show of that year a number of landscapes and flower studies and a portrait, done in striking grays, of an old man sitting in a garden. In the same year he did sketches for the settings and costumes of a Stravinsky ballet put on by Diaghileff in Monte Carlo.

Among other early works are "Vercingetorix," "The Abduction of Ganymede" (in two versions) and "View of the Acropolis." Characteristic of his later work are pastorals, landscapes, flower studies and innumerable bird pictures like "The Owl." A sort of bridge between the two periods is a self-portrait, done in 1922, in which the artist, straw-hatted, stands waist deep in a blooming flower garden.

✸   ✸

Bauchant is first and foremost a peasant from Touraine. His close relationship to the soil explains much of his painting, and the age-old myths of the soil are really his basic themes. It is not, however, out of peasant-like awe of chthonic power that he has been inspired to paint. Both cause and effect in his case are literary rather than primordial. In other words, it is not the rude, naked forces of nature that stir his

---

* Uhde's reference here may be to projects rather than to finished pictures, for there is a Bauchant "Battle of Palermo" dated 1925 and a "Proclamation of American Independence" dated 1926. (*Tr.*)

ANDRE BAUCHANT: FATHER TRUFFAULT

ANDRE BAUCHANT: THE OWL

emotions, but these forces dressed in legendary or historical garb. His patron saint would not be Dionysus of Delphi, in whose service the maenads made the slopes of Parnassus run red with blood, but Dionysus of Eleusis or Eleutheria, whose festivals ran red with wine. His poetic equivalent is not Aeschylus of the tragedies, but Theocritus of the idylls.

Nor is Bauchant a peasant out of Maupassant, subject to fierce emotions and ungovernable urges. He is rather a kindly, gentle peasant out of Jean Giono, and *Que ma joie demeure* might well be the motto of the pictures—even the ostensibly tragic ones—that he has based on the Bible, medieval romance and classic legend. He is fascinated by antiquity itself; he has an amateur antiquarian's interest in old and beautiful things. Once, while admiring some antique curios of mine, he told me how much he enjoyed rummaging around second-hand stores and junk shops. And, being the shrewd peasant that he is, with the typical peasant's respect for money, he added that he always wore his shabbiest clothes when he went on one of these rummaging expeditions.

There is no storm, stress and passion in his work. His descriptive pictures, ranging in period from the Greeks to Columbus, from Joan of Arc to Lafayette, are handled in light, flat colors, much like Quattrocento frescoes. The blood that spills is not black, like Agamemnon's, but rosy, and hence not too alarming. The wine that flows is not a heavy, red *Côtes du Rhône*, but a modest *vin du pays*, and hence not overpowering.

There is no overpowering expression of human experience in Bauchant, seizing the beholder with the grip of revelation. His work is rather an imaginative re-creation of literary experience, delicately displayed and epically designed. He writes on canvas with paints as a gifted story-teller writes on paper with ink, and no more transforms the canvas in the process than the writer does his sheet of paper. His work is individual and multiplex, but generally as interesting in terms of the "story" told as it is in terms of the art. The art is nevertheless there. The subtle, sensitive range of colors is extraordinary, and the stone-gray used in certain mountain scenes itself gives him rank as a painter. It is a genuine achievement.

★   ★

Like our other Primitives, Bauchant speaks from the heart, but his effects are greatly tempered by secondary, bookish influences. The only influence on Rousseau, Vivin and Séraphine came straight from the primary source of all influence. They were the more powerful and intense artists; he is more colorful and diverse. His pictures are especially welcome in an age of pseudo-sophistication, pretense and emptiness. He has given us the good earth again, and the myths which are its heritage.

ANDRE BAUCHANT: WINTER

ANDRE BAUCHANT: GETHSEMANE

CAMILLE BOMBOIS: STILL LIFE

CAMILLE BOMBOIS: THE RAILROAD STATION

C A M I L L E   B O M B O I S

Who is Camille Bombois? He used to be called a laborer who turned artist. Today he must be called an artist who was once a laborer by trade.

The difference is not merely verbal. It is fundamental. Bombois is above all an artist. He was an artist before he so much as put brush to canvas, when he was still chipping away at paving stones in the street. True, he has been a "common workman." But Spinoza was once a lens-polisher, Goethe a civil servant, Jasmin a hairdresser, Mallarmé a school-teacher, Claudel a diplomat.

Even a born artist needs opportunity and at least a minimum of food and drink. As a young man, Bombois had no opportunity, no money, no education to speak of. What he did have was an unusually powerful physique and the obligation to earn a living somehow. So he took up shovel, hammer and pick, and went to work.

Maximilien Gauthier has told the story in some detail. Born in Venarey-Les Laumes, near Troyes, in 1883, Bombois attended the village school for a few years. At the age of twelve, he left and went to work on a farm near Laroche. His gift for drawing was patent almost from the start, but the youth himself was more concerned with his gift of physical strength. Stocky and broad shouldered, he became the champion local wrestler, proudly matching his skill against that of professionals who visited the neighborhood with traveling circuses and carnivals. In due course, he turned professional strong-man himself, and toured the Haute-Saône and Haute-Marne, then quit and became a road-gang hand. Later he moved to Paris and married.

By 1907 he was working as a laborer on the Paris underground railway. There, in the dark tunnels of the city, he must have hungered for the

light in which his pictures are bathed. In any event, he soon found another job: manhandling huge rolls of newsprint in the pressroom of a
newspaper plant. This was a night job, and thus at last he had some spare
time during daylight hours in which he could begin to paint—only to
have his long struggle toward self-fulfillment interrupted by the first
World War. He served in the front lines from 1914 to the Armistice,
and won three awards for bravery in action.

By 1922 (he was then 39) Bombois had decided that painting was his
true career, and began displaying his work on the sidewalks of Montmartre. Numerous other fledgling artists did so too, but his attracted
attention almost immediately. Friendly notices appeared in a periodical
called *Rythme et Synthèse*, and a perceptive dealer named Mathot hung
a few of the pictures in the back room of his bric-a-brac shop on the
Rue des Martyrs. Before long every available Bombois had vanished from
both sidewalk and shop. They had been bought up by Madame Cecile
Grégory for her collection.

Even this, however, did not spell liberation for Bombois. He remained
a prisoner in a sense—bound no longer, to be sure, by the shackles of
a daily job, but still bound by those of circumstance and environment.
I once went to see him in his flat in a remote section of Paris. It was a
dreadful place, in a new, jerry-built, five-story house. The walls were
so thin that every sound was audible. Tenants waked in the morning to
the tinny blare of a neighbor's phonograph, and retired at night to the
tune of yawns, belches, lovers' groans and family quarrels. There is no
more terrible bondage than this.

Bombois, I realized, had not yet found the freedom he so richly
deserved. He found it finally by quitting Paris, which had given him his
great chance, and moving back to the country. Through the sale of his
pictures, he was able to make down-payment on a house and to start
retiring the mortgage by regular installments included in the rent. Soon
after he moved, I visited him again, and found a great artist who had
become a free man at last. He had triumphed over the full sum of adver-
sity. Now his hands, calloused by hard labor but still as sensitive as those
of a Perugino, were his to do with as he pleased. Now at last he had a
home—utterly prosaic in style, but bright and fresh inside, with his own
pictures hung on the walls and a special room in which he could paint.

Now he could lead the career for which he had been destined from the

CAMILLE BOMBOIS: THE CATHEDRAL OF ALBI

CAMILLE BOMBOIS: DANCER

start: that of a free man, an artist, a healthy lover of life, eager to demonstrate his love and endowed with magnificent means of self-expression. All this is easily enough explained. What is almost impossible to explain is the power and eloquence of the pictures.

✶   ✶

They are peculiarly virile and solid pictures—as natural and sensual as life itself is in villages and small towns. And it is life itself that interests Bombois—the primary energy and endless vitality of life, not secondary or temporary significances. When he paints a path, it leads somewhere. His bridges are substantial bridges; his churches seem to be built of actual brick and stone. His art is not an expression of sensibility *via* symbolism, but sensibility expressed *via* delight in literal fact and form.

The objects he paints are almost literal facts, and take on almost physical form by virtue of his magical sense of the third dimension. One can all but pace off the distance between any two given points in a Bombois scene, or measure the length of a bridge, the width of a footpath, the distance along a winding road. Bombois has become, indeed, one of the great masters of painted depth and space, more marvelous even than Carpaccio or Degas, and rivaled only by the old Dutch masters. Even such an early work as his view of the Laroche railroad station (in the Michelis collection) is an astonishing feat in this respect. There is full, tangible body to whatever Bombois draws, not simply length, breadth and surface. It is, once again, life that interests him—life that he can touch, grasp, fondle and embrace.

It follows that his wife, a ripe and Rubens-like woman, is his favorite model. A number of full-length nudes of Madame Bombois hang in their home. Even in her presence I have never felt uneasy when looking at them, as under such circumstances a visitor to the house might very well feel. They are altogether too hearty and natural to be in the least embarrassing because they are nudes.

Likewise among Bombois' favorite subjects are certain scenes from his boyhood and youth—especially water scenes. His father worked as a railroad hand, but before that had been a bargeman, and young Camille lived on the family barge until he was old enough to be sent to school. Hence his many river and canal views—scenes of boats drifting with the current, villages mirrored in placid streams, stagnant pools, water lilies, waterfalls. In some of these pictures—*e.g.*, a large canal scene with washerwomen grouped in the foreground—the calm expanse of water serves, like a snowy plain in Breughel, to draw the eye deeper and deeper into the distance. The horizon seems infinitely remote yet infinitely credible, thanks to the delicate facility of this "common workman's" hands.

His early pictures are generally in subdued colors resembling those of the old Dutch masters, though now and then there is a suggestion of the more modern range of Corot, and "The Cathedral at Albi" is altogether in the tonalities of Corot's Italian period. In later pictures Bombois' color sense undergoes a marked change. Recalling scenes from the circuses and carnivals he knew as a young man, he uses brilliant pinks, greens and blues, and a superb black glistens from the iron bar-bells the professional strong-man once toted triumphantly about the ring. In his landscapes, portraits and still-lifes alike, Bombois has become a brilliant colorist. His vigorous colors are but another evidence of his vigorous love of life.

There is a significant self-portrait in the Grenoble Museum. Bombois stands, palette in hand, before a picture on an easel. The picture is in the background, the artist himself (half-length) and his palette occupy the foreground. That is all one sees in the frame—and the palette, boldly splashed with a rainbow of colors, is the key to the whole.

As noted some pages back, there is also an artist-with-palette self-portrait by Rousseau. The Douanier stands by the Seine, a flag-bedecked ship and tall houses in the distance, a balloon floating overhead through a field of fantastic clouds. The key here, however, is not the palette's neat little pattern of color but the boldly-inscribed names of his two wives: *Clémence et Joséphine.*

The difference in these portraits is a measure of the difference in the emotional make-up of the two men. One lived and loved in a quaint, ceremonial world of his own creation. The other has broadened and intensified the world we all love and live in.

CAMILLE BOMBOIS: LANDSCAPE

CAMILLE BOMBOIS: THE CLEARING

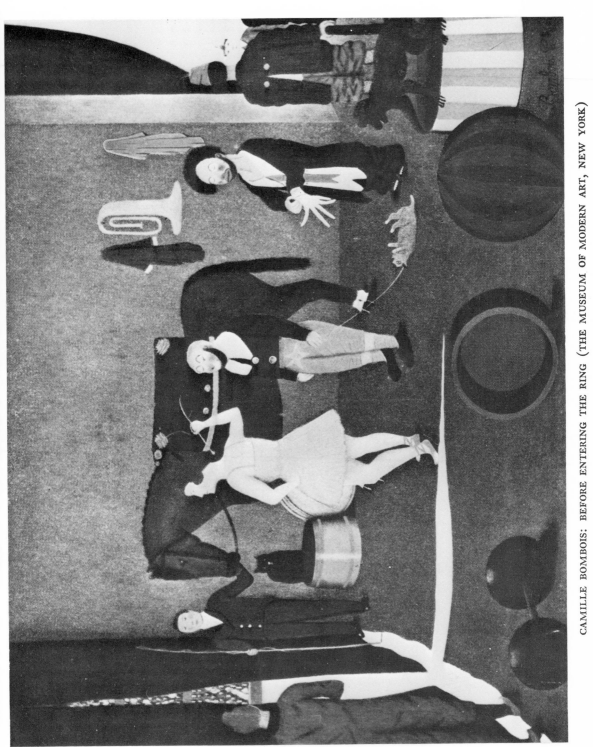

CAMILLE BOMBOIS: BEFORE ENTERING THE RING (THE MUSEUM OF MODERN ART, NEW YORK)

SERAPHINE DE SENLIS

About 1912 I went out to Senlis and rented a little place, consisting of two rooms and entry-hall, for 15 francs a month. I filled it with odds and ends of furniture, hung a few pictures on the walls, and thus had a hide-away convenient to Paris and yet remote from the Homeric wars then raging in Parisian art circles.

The placid Ile de France skies and peaceful life of the old province had always attracted me, and the old city of Senlis seemed the most placid and peaceful spot of all. Centuries before, Frankish invaders from the east must have felt much the same way, for they settled in the town and in time mingled their barbaric German genius with the prevailing Gallo-Roman. A fruit of this mingling was Senlis Cathedral, one of the earliest and finest Gothic structures in the Ile de France. Untamed Frankish energy, related to and perhaps even sprung from that of ancient Greece, provided the lift and soaring passion of the design. Its solidity and stability derived from the mature culture of the Gallo-Romans. Vertical and horizontal, as it were, fused into a new unity; dynamic creative enthusiasm blended with static heroism of form.

I know of no place where the Gothic synthesis is more nearly palpable than within the picturesque walled town of Senlis. Here, in a sense, the story of France began, likewise the history of its religion and the history of its kings. For Senlis was a royal residence during the Merovingian dynasty founded by Clovis I. Clovis, a convert to Christianity, made it a Christian center as well, with ultimately upwards of twenty churches. And, generations later, Senlis was a seat of the Capetian dynasty which was to rule the kingdom of France, after the election of Hugh Capet in A.D. 987, for 800 years.

But by 1912 the old town had long been asleep. Its quiet streets, desecrated churches, ruined chapels and gardens behind lichened walls lay dreaming dreams of the vanished Middle Ages. Little did I realize when I arrived that somewhere within this ancient silence was a talent which had brought the Middle Ages to life again—that here a simple housemaid had been inspired to re-create in her own way the sublime artistry of the Gothic. The medieval bells of Senlis were about to sound again, and I myself would have the great good fortune to be the first to hear them chime. With no suspicion of what lay in store, I moved into my rooms on the Place Lavarande.

★　　★

Of course I needed someone to keep the rooms clean, so I hired an old woman to come in by the day. Her name was Séraphine Louis, and she had been recommended as trustworthy. Aside from that, I knew nothing of her and paid no particular attention to her goings and comings. Indeed, I usually arranged to start off on my daily constitutional around the town when she arrived to sweep up.

One day, though, while visiting the home of a local family, I noticed a picture—a still-life so odd that the sight of it brought me up short. As I looked at it, spellbound, I suddenly realized that it was not only an odd picture but one of enormous artistic merit. It showed simply a heap of apples—but these apples were amazingly drawn, and handled in a solid, beautiful texture that would have captivated Cézanne. "For heaven's sake, who did this?" I asked. "Séraphine," I was told. "*Which* Séraphine?" "Why, Séraphine your housemaid. She's thinking of selling the picture to us, but if you like it, why don't you buy it? The price is 8 francs."

When Séraphine arrived to brush up the next morning, there was her still-life propped on a chair. "Ah," she said smiling, "I see Monsieur has my picture. Monsieur likes my picture?" I assured her that I did, and asked if she had painted any more. Eventually she brought me half a dozen more, each as amazing as the first. A veritable spiritual fervor and

88

SERAPHINE DE SENLIS: FRUITS AND FLOWERS

SERAPHINE DE SENLIS: LEAVES

medieval ardor seemed to suffuse them all. I made a point of showing them to friends whose artistic opinions I especially valued, and they were as deeply moved as I.

Then, in 1914, came the war. As I have already explained, my collection of pictures in Paris was auctioned off as enemy property, and the contents of my little place in Senlis were also sequestered and put up for public sale. I have never been able to find out who bought my Séraphines at the auction.

★   ★

After the war, when again established in Paris, I again longed for a suburban hideaway. Senlis was out of the question, so I took a small place in Chantilly, not far away, and furnished it with a few things I treasured especially. And there one day I read of an exhibit of local art on display in the Senlis Town Hall. My first thought, needless to say, was of Séraphine. Dropping everything, I got to Senlis as quickly as possible.

Despite the ravages of war, the old town had changed very little in thirteen years. The bells in most of its churches still hung mute. Its once-proud mansions and once-royal palaces were, as ever, apparently deserted, and the dully-glazed windows of the town jail stared out, as ever, like so many dead eyes. Its quaint streets were still quiet except for muffled traffic, the voices of occasional passers-by, the clank of a Spahi's sword as he hastened to the nearest brothel, the faint music of a boys' choir drifting in from St. Vincent's Abbey on the banks of the Nonette. A vast, venerable somnolence brooded over all, and smoke from the chimney pots rose straight into the cloudless Ile de France sky.

As for the Town Hall exhibit, it turned out to be, for the most part, the usual provincial display of amateurish oils, water colors and whatnot. But, staring glumly around the room, I saw at last what I had come to see: three large canvases of breathtaking power. They were all flower pieces of a sort—lilacs in a black vase, a cherry tree, grape vines laden with light and dark fruit. I stood rapt before them, and heard in the distance, miraculously, the long-hushed bells begin to chime: the bells of

St. Fraimbault, St. Aignan and Ste. Geneviève, of St. Hilaire, St. Martin and St. Etienne.

The exhibit closed a few weeks later. When the exhibitors came to collect their work, Séraphine was congratulated by the members of the committee, for she was the only one who had sold anything. In keeping with the dignity of the occasion, she wore black stockings and her shoes with patent-leather tips, and her best black holiday shawl.

The following day I came to pick up my pictures and take them back to Chantilly. The gentlemen of the committee congratulated me, as well, but with more than a little irony, or even pity, in their manner. As I was about to leave, one of them burst out, "Never can tell, sir, but maybe Paris will take pictures like those seriously some fine day. Maybe they'll become valuable. Never can tell!" I turned around and bowed, and the committeemen bowed in return.

★   ★

In a wretched little room a votive flame fluttered before a print of the Virgin Mary. As I came in, there stood Séraphine—tiny, withered, her eyes alight in the tired face under the fringe of faded hair. "Monsieur has come back," she said matter-of-factly. "It was Monsieur, I know, who bought my pictures at the Town Hall. Well, I no longer go out to do day's work for people. I paint, but I'm old and just a beginner and it's very hard to get along."

There was a sound at the door. Séraphine put a finger to her lips and inclined her head to listen. Someone knocked, knocked again and, receiving no answer, walked away. I looked at Séraphine questioningly. "Those wicked women," she whispered, "those wicked women come to insult me every day. They tell me I'm bad. They say I'm cheeky to try to paint when I'm only a poor, uneducated servant girl."

Poor and uneducated or not, from that day forward Séraphine had everything a painter could desire. She no longer needed to mix her colors with oil from the votive lamp on her mantlepiece. She had paints, oils, varnishes, brushes, even the heavy six-foot canvases which she said she needed particularly. A truck running between Paris and Senlis brought her the supplies.

She knew exactly what she wanted and what she didn't want—and she didn't want any of the pigments I sent. Somehow she found her own, and mixed them with a lacquer according to a formula of her own. She mixed them in secret and painted in secret. To prevent a visitor's catching her unawares, she had an involved system of locks and chains on her door, and posted a sign, *Mademoiselle Séraphine is not at home to callers*, at the foot of the stairs. In recent years more than one highly-trained artist has asked how Séraphine managed to produce her magnificent textures. I myself don't know, for I never saw her actually at work.

But however she managed it, her pictures seem to be the astounding product of centuries of skill. Her whole career, in fact, is astounding. To begin with, how did she, an old woman, find the strength simply to lift her six-foot canvases? They were heavy enough when new; when thickly overlaid with paints, they were heavier still. Moreover, whence came her impetus to paint, her desire for self-expression, a sense of color and form so confident as to imply a great and unbroken artistic tradition? The story of her life can be put into a few words. She was born in the village of Assy in 1864, tended the family cattle as a young girl, then came to Senlis and went into domestic service. She had never so much as set foot in Paris, twenty or thirty miles away.

It is easy to be misled by the apparently simplicity of her work. The subject matter may seem limited to a cluster of leaves, an assortment of fruit, a bouquet of flowers. But these leaves, fruits and flowers are Séraphine's portrait of royal France, of medieval Senlis, of divinity itself. The pictures are not mere casual, pleasant, innocent, peasant art. They are inspired and ecstatic art, and can be fully understood only if one regards the shepherdess of Assy as a sort of younger sister to the shepherdess of Domrémy. Séraphine brought to her work much the same sense of mission that inspired Joan at Rheims, and died in spiritual torture much as Joan died in physical torture at Rouen.

★　　★

She lived an unutterably lonely life. All dedicated artists, to be sure, are lonely to a degree. But most of them have friends or family on whom they can rely, or some other resources on which they can draw, if need be, for solace and justification. Manet, for example, at least realized that Velasquez and Goya too had been scorned in their time, and Corot knew of the experiences of Le Nain, Chardin and Guardi. Such artists, moreover, dealt with themes essentially familiar and appealing *per se*, rather than with those which Philistia was certain to dismiss as merely "crazy."

Séraphine had no range of theme. She worked courageously within the most restricted limits. She knew nothing of the history of the arts, and had no inkling of the relationship between her leaves, fruits and flowers and old Gothic tapestry or Gothic glass in cathedrals. A few decades earlier, Vincent Van Gogh had begun to work with much the same religious zeal and lonely sense of destiny; Séraphine had no inkling of him, either. In most respects, of course, their work is quite dissimilar. But both are distinguished by intense emotional fervor and extraordinary color harmonies. Van Gogh's blazing sunflowers and cypresses are products of the same strange botany as the trees and flowers of Séraphine.

★   ★

In the celestial hierarchy of the medieval church, the seraphim are highest of the nine angelic orders. What better name for the frail little woman of Senlis? Her pictures are not "logical" or "clever," but celestially intoxicated in the full medieval sense of the term. They are absolute inspiration, conceived on an inaccessible plane of ecstatic rapture. Rousseau, in his rapture, set a red sofa in the jungle for Yadwigha to rest upon. So Séraphine sometimes put shells on her trees instead of leaves, or drew the trees in the form of strange beasts of the sea. Foliage like hers never grew and never will grow. It represents a special ecology, as highly evolved and richly colored as sunlit stained glass, and as inimitable and unforgettable.

The form as well as the idea of Séraphine's pictures reflected ecstatic experience, but the actual painting was soberly planned and carried out.

SERAPHINE DE SENLIS: GRAPES

SERAPHINE DE SENLIS: THE TREE OF PARADISE

That is to say, however fierce and soul-shaking her inspiration, she was able to adapt it calmly to the surface of a canvas and the dimensions of a frame. She was a seeress and a psychotic but also a craftsman, with a fine sense of color, texture and composition, patiently weighing alternatives of harmony and design (and often asking my advice, as Rousseau had done) until the problems were solved. Once again, the Gothic art born of Frankish passion and Gallo-Roman patience bloomed in the person of Séraphine.

Her idiom may seem limited and her horizons restricted, when compared to Rousseau's or Vivin's. But if their work is the broader and fuller, hers has the greater dynamic force. It is ascetic, cloistered art, as simple as a folk song, yet it wells up as rapturously as the Song of Solomon, as richly sensuous as the solemn ceremonials of the Church. It is unique and incomparable, subject to none of the ordinary "laws" of painting, but strictly obedient to its own. To assess it in conventional terms of style, technique, intentions, etc., would be beside the point. Though an embodiment of art, it is more than that. It is an embodiment of Grace.

★   ★

Newspapers and art journals began to take notice of Séraphine during her last years, and a few discerning collectors began to buy her pictures. In short, the influence of Paris supplanted that of the "wicked women" who had knocked at the door in Senlis. In consequence, those who knocked now were friends and well-wishers. Once when I was there, the Mother Superior of the local hospital came to call, accompanied by several respectable old ladies, and there was much talking and laughing over a poem Séraphine had once written and had insisted upon reading aloud. Séraphine welcomed such guests and other signs of success as though she had expected them all along. No one believed more firmly than she in her own genius—not out of self-esteem, but because she felt, as in his case Rousseau had felt, that God was guiding her hand.

Now and then she would come to Chantilly to call on me, covering the 9 kilometers on foot. Normally she carried a bag packed with food and wine, and a little stool on which to sit by the roadside when she became weary. She was not always pleased with what she found when she arrived. The sight of one of her pictures set temporarily on the floor upset her a great deal; she warned me earnestly that rats and mice might get at it. And the sight of Vivin's pictures upset her wherever they were. Once she remarked rather crossly, as she examined one at close range, "Do you mean to say this was painted by hand?"

★   ★

The general business depression of the 1930's affected me as it did everyone else. When my resources began to dwindle, I was forced to ask Séraphine to economize wherever she could. But she lived, as had the Douanier before her, in a world of her own. She had no real understanding of what I meant. Day after day she continued to buy things she had no earthly use for: furniture, carpets, dozens of heavily-ornamented silver forks and knives. She rented additional rooms, ran up debts, ordered large and expensively carved frames. She was sure she was rich, and her head swam with dreams of vast sales and international renown.

When the plain truth finally struck home, she had no inner resistance left. It had been used up, exhausted, lavishly spent on her work. What remained of her genius and heroism was merely a worn-out body and a distraught mind. She began going from house to house in Senlis, prophesying the end of the world—and never realizing that it was her own world that was coming to an end. Finally she was committed to the insane asylum at Clermont, and there she died in 1934.

The last large painting she did in Senlis shows no sign of this tragic end. It is a fragile network of foliage done in tints of light green, pink, yellow and gray. After her death I discovered it in a Senlis auction room, stuck in a corner and covered with dust. No one in town had cared enough, or been courageous enough, to put in a bid for a picture by that crazy old servant girl.

SERAPHINE DE SENLIS: FLOWERING TREE

TABLE OF ILLUSTRATIONS

This book is the English language edition of the original German edition, published by Atlantis Verlag A G, Zurich, in 1947.

The text has been condensed by the translator and part of the introduction omitted. Two color reproductions, Rousseau's "Waterfall" and Bombois' "Before Entering the Ring," have been added.

This book was manufactured in the U.S.A. for the Quadrangle
Press, Incorporated during the spring of 1949. Both the text, set in
Janson type, and the illustrations were printed by the Ram Press
in New York. The book was bound by John M. Gettler, also in
New York.